The Alternative Rock Scene

The Stars ♪ The Fans ♪ The Music

Wendy S. Mead

Enslow Publishers, Inc.
40 Industrial Road
Box 398
Berkeley Heights, NJ 07922
USA

http://www.enslow.com

Library of Congress Cataloging-in-Publication Data
Mead, Wendy.
  The alternative rock scene : the stars, the fans, the music / Wendy S. Mead.
     p. cm. — (The music scene)
  Includes bibliographical references and index.
  Summary: "Read about the music, stars, clothes, contracts, and world of alternative rock music"—Provided by publisher.
  ISBN-13: 978-0-7660-3401-3
  ISBN-10: 0-7660-3401-1
  1. Alternative rock music—History and criticism—Juvenile literature. I. Title.
  ML3534.M475 2009
  782.42166—dc22

                              2008048015

Printed in the United States of America

10 9 8 7 6 5 4 3 2 1

To Our Readers:
This text has not been authorized by the musicians or bands mentioned throughout this book.

    We have done our best to make sure all Internet addresses in this book were active and appropriate when we went to press. However, the author and the publisher have no control over and assume no liability for the material available on those Internet sites or on other Web sites they may link to. Any comments or suggestions can be sent by e-mail to comments@enslow.com or to the address on the back cover.

♻ Enslow Publishers, Inc., is committed to printing our books on recycled paper. The paper in every book contains 10% to 30% post-consumer waste (PCW). The cover board on the outside of each book contains 100% PCW. Our goal is to do our part to help young people and the environment too!

Cover Photo Credit: Getty Images
Interior Photo Credits: Alamy/Photos 12, p. 22; Alamy/Jupiter Images/Creatas, p. 35; AP Photo/Mark Davis, p. 36; AP Photo/Ric Feld, p. 41; Chris Berkey, p. 12; Corbis/Yorick Jansens/epa, p. 16; Corbis/Steve Appleford, p. 31; Corbis/Tim Mosenfelder, p. 34; Getty Images/Evan Agostini, p. 23; The Image Works/Francis Dean/Dean Pictures, p. 10; The Image Works/Nancy Richmond, p. 18; The Image Works/Jeff Greenberg, p. 38; Landov/Yui Mok/PA Photos, p. 2; Landov/Michael Germana/SSI Photo, p. 11; Landov/Mitch Dumke/Reuters, p. 20; Landov/Phil McCarten/Reuters, p. 21; Landov/Mike Blake/Reuters, p. 26; Photolibrary.com/Index Stock Imagery/Lauree Feldman, p. 25; Retna Ltd./Kelly A. Swift, pp. 1, 15, 27; Retna Ltd./Phil Bourne/Retna Pictures, p. 4; Retna Ltd./Robb D. Cohen, pp. 5, 6; Retna Ltd./Kevin Estrada, p. 9; Retna Ltd./Suzan/PA Photos, p. 14; Retna Ltd./Ashley Maile, p. 17; Retna Ltd./Ian Tilton, p. 24; Retna Ltd./Richard E. Aaron, p. 28; Retna Ltd./George Bodnar, p. 29; Retna Ltd./RD/Leon/Retna Digital, p. 32; Retna Ltd./David Atlas, p. 37; UrbanImage.tv/Adrian Boot, p. 8.

Cover: Vampire Weekend performs at a festival in Tennessee in 2008.

Right: Thom Yorke of the Grammy-winning band Radiohead takes the stage at Victoria Park in London.

Contents

1 *Hot Stuff*

Dare to be different? That's what alternative rockers do. They make all kinds of music, from fast and furious to moody and mellow. But they stand united on one thing. Their music doesn't sound like your typical pop song.

HOT *Indie Band*

Vampire Weekend is a band of four college friends. Their unique sound includes bits of 1980s pop and traditional African music. The result is a catchy type of indie rock.

The indie band Vampire Weekend plays live at the Forum in London.

4

HOT *Punk Band*

Another up-and-coming band is *Against Me!* This Florida band has ramped up its punk-folk sound to create edgier music. The foursome shakes things up with powerful rhythms and lyrics.

If you're looking for a harder rock sound, check out Against Me!

HOT *Emo Band*

Do you like dark lyrics and driving guitars? Check out *My Chemical Romance*. They are one of the top emo acts today. There are two Way brothers in My Chemical Romance. *Gerard Way* is the band's front man. *Mikey Way* plays bass.

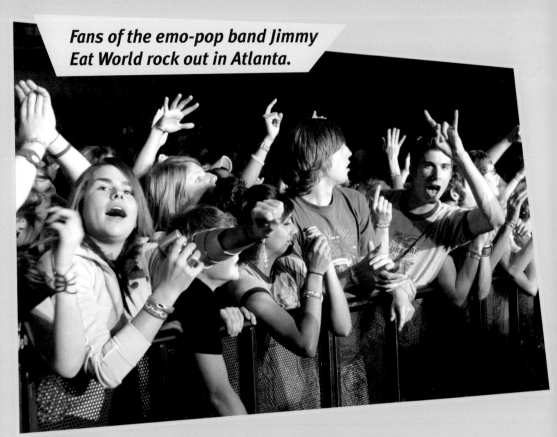

Fans of the emo-pop band Jimmy Eat World rock out in Atlanta.

② "I'm Your Biggest Fan!"

There are nearly as many types of fans as there are types of alternative music. Some are into the goth-punk sounds of *AFI*. Others cannot get enough of the emo-pop of *Jimmy Eat World*. Teenagers are some of the most diehard fans. The Warped Tour, for instance, is popular with teenage guys.

College Goes Indie

Indie music is huge with college students. They want to hear original sounds, not the same old pop tunes. Many can listen to their school's radio station to check out the latest in indie. College DJs try to play new music and small bands. For example, Evergreen State College's KAOS station has pledged to play 80 percent independent music.[1] Some students also tune in to mtvU, the college version of MTV.

Alternative Adults

A lot of adults like alternative rock, too. Many grew up when punk exploded in the 1970s, or they were college students when Seattle's grunge sound arrived in the 1990s. These fans want to hear some of alternative's early artists. They tune in for songs by **Pearl Jam**, **Nirvana**, the **Red Hot Chili Peppers**, and **Green Day**.

Straight to the Fans

In 2007, **Radiohead** first released their seventh album, *In Rainbows*, as a download on their Web site. Fans flocked to their computers. In 2009, *In Rainbows* won the Grammy Award for Best Alternative Music Album.

3 Ultimate Style

Not everyone wearing a long, dark trench coat is goth. Sure, goths like to wear black. But silver, purple, and dark red are also part of the style.[2]

Some goths dress up as if it's still the 1800s. They wear long dresses or fancy suits made of velvet, lace, or satin.[3] Others prefer a more modern look, such as a dark T-shirt and boots.

Punk *Then and Now*

The early days of punk were all about rough and ragged clothes. The *Ramones* and the *Clash* liked leather jackets. Today it's still about looking like you don't care. Leather, ripped T-shirts, and black boots are popular choices for punks.

The Clash helped define punk style.

Go Grunge

It's about the music, not the clothes. That feeling was a big part of the 1990s grunge rock scene. The artists did not dress to impress. *Eddie Vedder* of Pearl Jam often wore old flannel shirts, faded T-shirts, and jeans.

Fancy Pants

Some alternative bands like to dress formally. The members of the Swedish band the *Hives* appear in matching suits. *Interpol*'s members often wear suits and ties.

Eddie Vedder of Pearl Jam sports the just-rolled-out-of-bed look of grunge rock at the Lollapalooza festival in 1992.

The hair-raising mohawk is a classic punk style.

Extreme *Hair Makeover*

Alternative hairstyles are anything but boring. A classic punk look is the mohawk. Punks shave off all their hair except for one strip in the center. Then they spike up the strip.

In a faux-hawk, most of the hair is cut close to the head. The rest is left longer so that it can be spiked up.

Other fans and artists use hair dye to make a statement. They add bright colors or bold stripes to their hair. Many goths dye their hair black, dark purple, or blue.

10

Guy-Liner

Makeup is key for alternative rockers. A dark line around the eyes is almost a given. **Pete Wentz**, the bassist for **Fall Out Boy**, is known for this look. It is sometimes called guy-liner.

Check out the hands of your favorite performers. You're bound to see dark nail polish. Black, gray, and deep red are the most popular colors.

Rocker Pete Wentz never leaves home without his guy-liner.

Collars, Cuffs, and Crosses

Jewelry is an important part of alternative style. Punks wear heavy metal—thick chains and even dog collars. Goth girls often wear necklaces with symbols hanging from them.

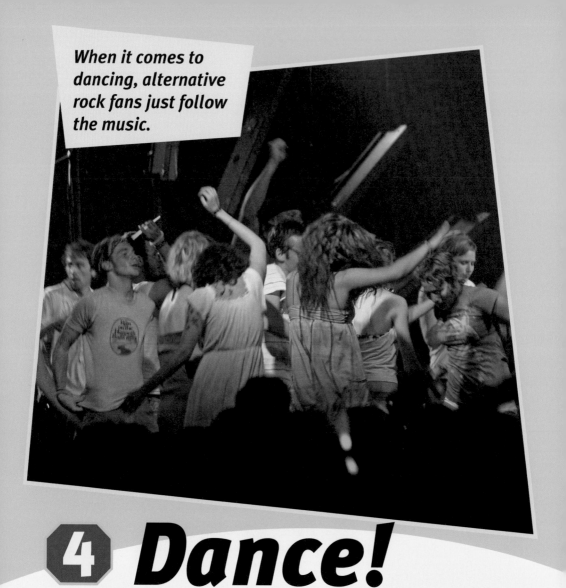

When it comes to dancing, alternative rock fans just follow the music.

4 Dance!

Alternative music has no formal dance steps. It's about doing what you feel.

Slam Dancing

With its revved-up speed and energy, punk rock really gets the crowd going. You can often find people slam dancing. They wave their arms and kick their legs. Sometimes they crash into each other. There may even be some pushing—but it's all in fun. The dancers are just reacting to the driving sound around them.

Do You Pogo?

Other punks pogo, or jump up and down. This move was probably created by **Sid Vicious** of the **Sex Pistols** in the 1970s.[4] Vicious started jumping up and down when he couldn't see a band at a show. He later used this move as a performer. Many punks still pogo today.

Moving, Shoegaze Style

Some alternative music requires a more laid-back approach. Shoegaze music is a type of rock from Britain in the 1980s and 1990s. Shoegazers slowly swayed side to side and looked down at the ground. Shoegazing still happens at shows by **Air Formation**, **Sonic Youth**, and the **Daysleepers**.

When the Foo Fighters take to the road, it's a major production!

5 On the Road

When the **Foo Fighters** hit the road, they do not pack light. It takes several buses to lug their gear. For starters, there are four band members. Then add on a road crew and extra musicians. The band's families often come along for the ride, too.

Sometimes artists get sick on the road. During their 2008 tour, Foo Fighters lead singer **Dave Grohl** got the flu. The band had to cancel a concert. On the band's blog, Grohl wrote, "Anyone who knows this band knows we rarely ever cancel gigs. . . . Well, yours truly is down for the count."[5]

The Foo Fighters get their name from a military term for an unidentified flying object, or UFO.

The Foo Fighters usually play at arenas and large concert halls. On the day of the show, the band's crew sets everything up. They put up the lights and get the sound system and instruments ready. The band visits the arena to make sure everything is all set for the show.

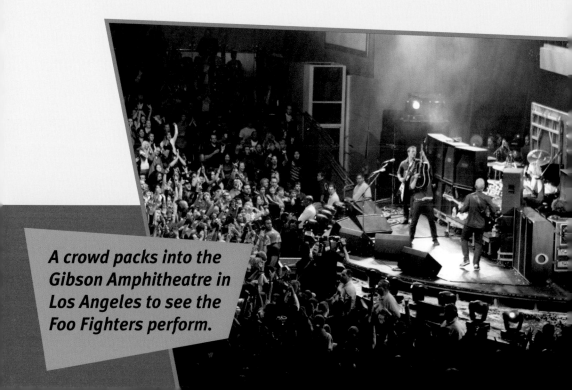

A crowd packs into the Gibson Amphitheatre in Los Angeles to see the Foo Fighters perform.

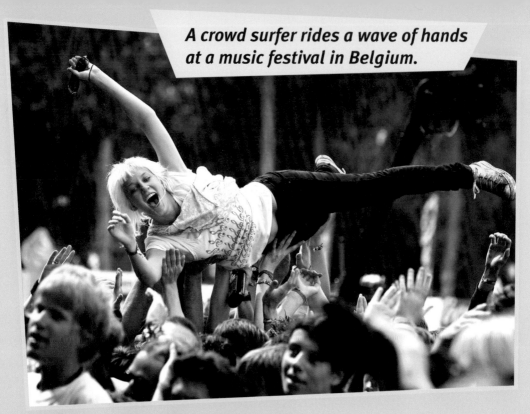

A crowd surfer rides a wave of hands at a music festival in Belgium.

6 Live!

In the Pit

Going to an alternative rock show can be like doing extreme sports. There is a swarm of people in the mosh pit. They bounce off each other as the band plays.

The mosh pit has its hazards, though. Fans often get hit by a flying elbow or two. If you enter the pit, wear sturdy shoes. And stand up quickly if you fall down so you don't get stepped on!

Rising Above the Rest

Crowd surfing is another popular stunt. Fans "ride" on top of the audience as they get passed along. Usually surfers move along just fine, but sometimes they get dropped. For instance, one teenager got a neck injury while crowd surfing at a concert in Florida.[6]

Keeping Set Lists

Some fans keep set lists for each concert. They write the title of every song that a band plays. They compare lists from the band's other shows to learn which songs get played the most. Some bands, like the **Red Hot Chili Peppers**, post set lists on their Web sites.

A fan shows off his set list at a concert.

⑦ *Ear Candy*

Ready to listen? The radio is a good place to start. Your area might have an alternative rock station. College stations are a good bet, too. They are more likely to put indie artists and other lesser-known groups on the air. You can find alternative rock on satellite radio. You can also listen to alternative radio stations on the Internet.

A DJ is surrounded by CDs at a college radio station in Durango, Colorado.

Online *Finds*

Podcasts are another way to tune in. *Alternative Press* magazine has a podcast that includes interviews with bands such as **Yellowcard**, **Cobra Starship**, and **As I Lay Dying**. On Indiefeed's Web site, you can subscribe to a podcast with new songs from different indie artists.

Some bands post music files on their Web sites. When you want to get a song for your own collection, buy it through online music sites such as iTunes. That way you can support your favorite bands.

On *TV*

Check out alternative video shows on cable television. Fuse has a show called *The Dive* for up-and-coming artists. On MTV2 there's *Subterranean*, a weekly show. *Subterranean* also has its own blog.

Fall Out Boy poses for a photo at an inaugural ball in Washington, D.C., in January 2009.

8 *Hottest Videos*

Some of the best music videos are made by bands that don't take themselves too seriously.

In "See You at the Lights," the *1990s* go wild with animated versions of themselves. Clay figures of this Scottish trio act out the song. For most of the video, the characters play around on a rooftop.

In "Thnks fr th Mmrs," *Fall Out Boy* gets bossed around by a group of chimpanzees. The video's director, Shawn Chimp, and the rest of his crew create problems for the band. For example, the director doesn't like lead singer

Patrick Vaughn Stump, but he does like bassist ***Pete Wentz***'s girlfriend. By the end of the video, Wentz loses his girl to the chimp.

Paramore goes back to high school in "Misery Business." In the video, a girl in a tight dress walks through the halls of a school. She seems to be out for revenge, as she pushes some cheerleaders out of her way. She cuts a girl's braid off and twists a guy's arm. She even kisses someone else's boyfriend. In the end, lead singer ***Hayley Williams*** finally stops her.

The members of Paramore try not to take themselves too seriously.

9 On the Big Screen

Next time you go to the movies, listen to the music. Chances are you'll hear some of your favorite alternative rock. Director Zach Braff selected all the songs for his 2004 film *Garden State*. It is about a young actor who returns home to New Jersey for his mother's funeral. The alternative music sets the mood for the film. "Some of the songs were actually written into the script," Braff said.[7]

Director Zach Braff (right) set the mood of his film **Garden State** *with a soundtrack of alternative rock.*

*Some alternative musicians are actors, too. **Kim Gordon** from **Sonic Youth** has appeared in several films and on the television series* Gilmore Girls.

The *Garden State* soundtrack helped the careers of the artists, including **Iron and Wine** and the **Shins**. The Shins' album *Oh, Inverted World* went on to sell more than a half million copies.

Action-Packed Alternative

Bands like **Panic at the Disco**, **Coheed and Cambria**, and the **All-American Rejects** added energy to the action film *Snakes on the Plane* (2006). In the movie, Samuel L. Jackson plays an FBI agent. His mission is to take a witness to a trial. To survive the trip, he has to fight a plane full of deadly snakes.

🔟 *First Moments*

Bands in the Seattle area started a new style of alternative music in the late 1980s. Borrowing from heavy metal and punk, the style was called grunge. One of the major grunge acts was **Nirvana**. The group released their first song, "Love Buzz," in 1987. Then Nirvana hit it big with their 1991 album, *Nevermind*.

Nirvana's song "Smells Like Teen Spirit" brought alternative rock to the mainstream. The song reached the top of the pop charts. Soon listeners were checking out other grunge bands, like **Pearl Jam** and **Soundgarden**.

Kurt Cobain (left), lead singer of Nirvana, became the symbol of a generation of alternative rock artists.

24

CBGB: *Home to Punk*

Before grunge there was punk. No place showed off punk's emerging sound better than the New York City club CBGB. The **Ramones** started playing their short, manic songs there around 1975. "We were a Bizarro-world version of the Beatles," explained Joey Ramone, the group's lead singer.[8] CBGB booked other up-and-coming punk bands, such as **Talking Heads** and **Blondie**.

Made in the Garage

*Garage bands emerged in the mid-1960s. They played a raw, simple style of rock. One of the most famous garage bands was the **Kingsmen**. They scored a big hit with "Louie, Louie" in 1963.*

Many of alternative rock's pioneers got their start at the New York City club CBGB.

11 Spreading Like Wildfire

Since the 1970s, alternative rock has caught on in a big way. New artists and events are sprouting up everywhere!

As Heard on TV

Some bands catch big breaks on the small screen. *Grey's Anatomy*, *The Hills*, and other television shows use alternative music. The **Postal Service** and the **Fray** have gained new fans this way.

Alternative music also catches on through TV commercials. **Feist**'s song "1234" became a big hit because of a 2007 iPod ad.[9]

Feist became a household name when her song "1234" appeared in a TV commercial.

Fans enjoy a fairyland atmosphere at the Coachella Valley Music and Arts Festival.

Festival *Fever*

Music festivals win over thousands of new alternative rock fans. Traveling shows like the Warped Tour offer a whole day's worth of bands.

If you're up for a road trip, check out a festival. California hosts the Coachella Valley Music and Arts Festival. The event brings together generations of alternative fans. Classic acts such as the **Breeders** and newer groups like **Les Savy Fav** have appeared at the event.

*New wave—a relative of punk—is back. Listen to the **Cure**, and then listen to **Arcade Fire**. Now try playing **Joy Division** and then **Interpol**.*

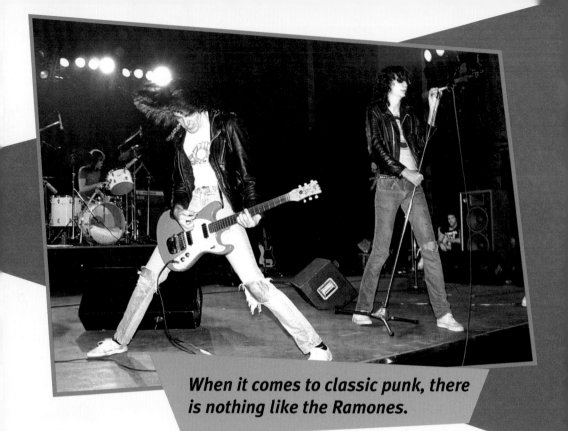

When it comes to classic punk, there is nothing like the Ramones.

⑫ *Not So Simple*

There seem to be endless terms to describe alternative music. All these words can make your head spin. Here are some ways to tell them apart.

All Sorts of Punk

The word *punk* usually refers to the original punk bands of the 1970s—the **Sex Pistols**, the **Clash**, and the **Ramones**. Punk also describes new bands that sound like the classic groups. **Green Day** is an example of today's punk.

Then there is post-punk, which was inspired by punk but went in different directions. The **Cure** and **Pere Ubu** are post-punk groups.

Punk-pop music blends both styles. It uses some of punk's fierceness in more mainstream song styles.

Goth is considered post-punk. Some of the early goth bands were Siouxsie and the Banshees, Sisters of Mercy (above), and Gene Loves Jezebel.

Understanding Indie

Indie stands for independent music—music made by artists working on their own or with a small record label. Indie comes in a variety of flavors. There's indie pop, which is more upbeat than indie rock. Lo-fi bands take indie to its most basic level. Their music has a rough, homemade quality.

⬡13 *The Studios*

To make a new album, most alternative bands head into the studio. Some go to big studios with lots of equipment. Others live by the indie ideal of DIY—do it yourself.

The *Red Hot Chili Peppers*, *Talking Heads*, and *My Chemical Romance* have recorded at Eldorado Recording Studios near Los Angeles. Travel up the California coast and you'll find Studio 880 in Oakland. Punk pioneer *Iggy Pop* of the *Stooges* and later-day punks *Green Day* captured some of their songs here.

The Icelandic band Sigur Ros made their own studio in an old building with an indoor swimming pool. "It's a really peaceful place. It didn't take long to set up because we worked really hard," said lead singer Jonsi Birgisson.[10]

Indie Artists at Work

Some indie bands are all about making music on their own. *The Walkmen* started the Marcata Recording Studio so that they could make music their own way. They opened up their space to other groups, including the *Kills*.

Alison Sudol of the band A Fine Frenzy records her debut album, One Cell in the Sea, *at Eldorado Studios.*

14 *Tale of a Contract*

Getting a recording contract takes talent, hard work, and luck. **Paramore** started out when lead singer **Hayley Williams** was in her early teens. Williams moved from Mississippi to Tennessee in 2002. There she met brothers **Josh** and **Zac Farro** at a program for home-schooled kids.

In 2005, Paramore scored their first record contract with John Janick, founder of the label Fueled by Ramen.

All Kinds of Harmony

The friends started playing together. Hayley took on the vocals, Josh the guitar, and Zac the drums. Williams brought in her friend **Jeremy Davis** to play bass. Paramore began developing a powerful punk-pop sound.

Getting the Gigs

Paramore started playing gigs in 2004. One of their first performances was in nearby Nashville. At a concert in Florida in early 2005, they were spotted by **John Janick**, founder of the Fueled by Ramen record label. After signing a record deal with him, Paramore went to work on their first album. *All We Know Is Falling* was released in the summer of 2005. Williams says, "Fueled By Ramen has been amazing to us. So many kids started checking us out because our name is on their roster. It's like a big family; we all share such a massive unit of fans."[11]

Paramore went on tour to promote their album. They played with the alternative pop band **Simple Plan** and the indie act **Straylight Run**. Paramore won over tons of fans at big festivals, such as the Warped Tour and the Bamboozle.

15 *Take One!*

Making an album can take anywhere from days to years. *Bloc Party* took more than a year to record their album *A Weekend in the City.* First the band came up with song ideas. The next step was growing those ideas into full songs. Then they made a demo—a sample recording.[12]

Hitting the Studio

Bloc Party recorded the album's songs in several different studios. They worked with producer *Jacknife Lee*. The producer and the band often go and back forth about a song.

They might rewrite the lyrics or change parts of the music. They keep working until they are happy with the song.

Every day in the studio is different. On one day, the whole band might record the instrumental tracks. The next day, the lead singer might work with the producer and the engineer to put down vocal tracks.

Sometimes bands record with guest musicians. For example, a group of string players helped give a lush feeling to **Bloc Party**'s "Where Is Home?"

A Bit of Polish

The songs go through a final step called mixing. An engineer puts together the tracks and makes adjustments. Then the engineer polishes up the tracks so they sound clean and smooth.

An engineer works at the sound board in a recording studio.

16 Alternative Rock in Action

For alternative rock artists, music is not just about bringing in money. Many bands give their time and money to help people in need.

End War in Africa

Check out *Instant Karma: The Amnesty International Campaign to Save Darfur*. This album was created to help stop the fighting in Darfur. Different groups in this area of

Snow Patrol was one of several bands to record a track for *Instant Karma: The Amnesty International Campaign to Save Darfur.* This album was recorded to help people suffering from violence in Darfur, an area of Sudan, Africa.

Sudan, Africa, have been battling each other for years. More than two million people have been forced out of their homes.

Groups such as **Green Day** and **Snow Patrol** recorded songs for *Instant Karma*. They did their own versions of songs by rock legend **John Lennon** for the project.

A Cure for Cancer

Andrew McMahon, the lead singer of **Jack's Mannequin**, started the Dear Jack Foundation. In 2005 McMahon learned that he had leukemia, a type of cancer. After getting treatment, McMahon was able to beat the disease. McMahon's foundation raises money for cancer research. "I feel an intense personal obligation . . . to raise both money and awareness for the countless young people who are being diagnosed with similar blood diseases," he said.[13]

Leukemia survivor Andrew McMahon raises money to fight cancer.

37

A high school rock band performs at an event in Miami Beach, Florida.

17 Get into It

Now that you know all about alternative rock, it's time to get into it!

Instruments of Rock

Learning to play an instrument is one way to get into the scene. The guitar is a popular choice. *Kazu Makino* asked musician *Amedeo Pace* for guitar lessons. The lessons must have

gone well. The two ended up forming the band
Blonde Redhead with Pace's twin brother **Simone**
on drums.[14]

Singing Your Way

Most alternative rock singers don't have any
formal training. But sometimes performers
get a little professional help on a song or even
an entire album. **Thursday**'s lead singer, **Geoff
Rickly**, worked with a vocal coach for his
2006 album *A City by the Light Divided*.[15] Vocal
training can be a good way to learn how to
perform live without hurting your voice.

Street Teams

Not a singer? Not interested in playing an
instrument? No problem. You can still get
involved. Many alternative bands and record
labels have street teams. As a member of a
street team, you help get the word out about
a band. This may mean hanging up posters
for a show. Or you might tell your friends
about the band's latest album. In return, the
band might give you free downloads, posters,
stickers, or other gifts.

18 *For a Living*

There are many **behind-the-scenes jobs** in alternative rock. Some people work for record companies as artist and repertoire representatives, or A&R reps. A&R reps are always on the lookout for great bands. They go to a lot of shows and clubs to discover new talent.

John Feldmann is the lead singer and guitarist of the punk band **Goldfinger**. Now he is also an A&R rep for Warner Bros. Records. Feldmann has signed contracts with such bands as the **Used**. To be a successful A&R rep, you need to be a good talker, listener, and negotiator.

Be the DJ

Being a radio DJ is another good job for alternative fans. DJs do more than play music. They talk about the bands and the songs. Sometimes DJs deliver news on the air or host special events for the radio station.

Becoming a DJ is a great way to turn your passion for music into a career.

Many DJs start out with a part-time gig for a local station. Others, such as **Les Aaron**, start out playing music in clubs. Aaron was inspired by **John Peel**, a legendary British DJ. "He would play bands that he liked to play," Aaron said.[16] Aaron does exactly that in his weekly alternative rock program, *New Music Sunday*.

Write It Up

Another great way to go alternative is to write about the scene. You can write about albums and concerts for a newspaper, a Web site, or a magazine. Official fan clubs need talented writers to share news about bands.

Glossary

blog—An online personal journal.

demo—A sample music recording that artists use to try and get gigs or record contracts.

emo—A musical style with lyrics about personal events and feelings.

engineer—A professional who works with the recording equipment in a studio.

goth—A style of music known for its lush, dark sound and poetic lyrics; also, the culture associated with the music.

grunge—A musical movement that blended punk and heavy metal to create its own unique, murky style.

indie—Music made independently, not by a large record company.

indie pop—A type of independent music that has a catchier, often softer quality than indie rock.

lo-fi—A style of independent music that uses old equipment to make music that sounds like it was created at home instead of in a studio.

mainstream—Leading trends, bands, and styles in pop culture.

manic—Very active and filled with energy.

mixing—Blending different music recordings into one version of a song.

Time Line

1968 The MC5 earned national attention with their first album, *Kick Out the Jams*, recorded in Detroit.

1973 The Stooges release *Raw Power*, which inspires the punk movement that soon follows.

1975 The New York City punk scene starts to emerge with appearances by the Ramones and other bands at the famed club CBGBs.

1977 The Sex Pistols release their first album in Britain.

1979 Bauhaus releases the first goth song, "Bela Lugosi's Dead."

1980s New wave music becomes popular.

1982 The Clash releases *Combat Rock*, their most popular album.

1991 Nirvana reaches the top of the charts with their album *Nevermind*, sparking the popularity of grunge music.

1992 The Red Hot Chili Peppers emerge as one of the top alternative acts of the year.

1993 Radiohead first makes it big with the song "Creep."

1994 Sunny Day Real Estate's first album, *Diary*, helps draw fans to the sounds of emo.

1995 The first Warped Tour takes place.

1996 The indie record label Fueled by Ramen is founded.

1998 The members of Interpol start playing together.

2002 The emo band Fall Out Boy is formed.

2004 The *Garden State* soundtrack helps launch the career of the Shins and several other indie artists.

2005 Paramore performs on the Warped Tour for the first time.

2008 Vampire Weekend releases their first album.

2009 Radiohead takes home a Grammy Award for their album *In Rainbows.*

Time Line

1968 The MC5 earned national attention with their first album, *Kick Out the Jams*, recorded in Detroit.

1973 The Stooges release *Raw Power*, which inspires the punk movement that soon follows.

1975 The New York City punk scene starts to emerge with appearances by the Ramones and other bands at the famed club CBGBs.

1977 The Sex Pistols release their first album in Britain.

1979 Bauhaus releases the first goth song, "Bela Lugosi's Dead."

1980s New wave music becomes popular.

1982 The Clash releases *Combat Rock*, their most popular album.

1991 Nirvana reaches the top of the charts with their album *Nevermind*, sparking the popularity of grunge music.

1992 The Red Hot Chili Peppers emerge as one of the top alternative acts of the year.

1993 Radiohead first makes it big with the song "Creep."

1994 Sunny Day Real Estate's first album, *Diary*, helps draw fans to the sounds of emo.

1995 The first Warped Tour takes place.

1996 The indie record label Fueled by Ramen is founded.

1998 The members of Interpol start playing together.

2002 The emo band Fall Out Boy is formed.

2004 The *Garden State* soundtrack helps launch the career of the Shins and several other indie artists.

2005 Paramore performs on the Warped Tour for the first time.

2008 Vampire Weekend releases their first album.

2009 Radiohead takes home a Grammy Award for their album *In Rainbows.*

End Notes

1. "Independent Music," *KAOS 89.3 FM*, December 15, 2007, <http://kaos.evergreen.edu/programs/music_policy.html> (March 20, 2008).

2. Nancy Kilpatrick, *The Goth Bible* (New York: St. Martin's Press, 2004), pp. 38–40.

3. Ibid, pp. 31–33.

4. Steve Huey, "Sid Vicious," *VH1.com*, n.d., <http://www.vh1.com/artists/az/vicious_sid/bio.jhtml> (January 2, 2008).

5. Dave Grohl, "Sick as a Dog," *Long Blog to Ruin*, n.d., <http://www.foofightersblog.com/2008/01/sick-as-a-dog.php> (February 3, 2008).

6. Chris Tisch, "Park Event's Success Comes at a Price," *St. Petersburg Times Online*, December 4, 2001, <http://www.sptimes.com/News/120401/news_pf/NorthPinellas/Park_event_s_success_.shtml> (October 27, 2008).

7. Chris Morris, "'Garden' Statement," *Hollywood Reporter*, International Edition, Vol. 387, Issue 15, January 7, 2005 (Accessed through the EBSCOhost MasterFile Premier Database).

8. Mark Blaine, editor, *Punk: The Whole Story* (New York: DK Publishing, 2006), p. 52.

9. Josh Rabinowitz, "Selling In: Song Placements Are About More Than Just sales," *Billboard*, March 15, 2008, p.13.

10. Mark Pytlik, "Sigur Ros," *Sound on Sound*, July 2002, <http://www.soundonsound.com/sos/Jul02/articles/sigurros.asp> (December 5, 2007).

11. "Paramore Band Info," *Paramore*, n.d., <http://www.paramore.net/about> (August 10, 2008).

12. Gordon Moakes, "The Record," *Bloc Party*, December 19, 2006, <http://www.blocparty.com/band.php> (January 7, 2008).

13. Andrew McMahon, *Dear Jack Foundation*, n.d., <http://www .dearjackfoundation.com/index.php> (November 30, 2007).

14. Brian Palmer, "Blonde Redhead," *Thrasher*, February 2008, p. 188.

15. Barry Walters, "Thursday: A City By the Light Divided," *Rolling Stone*, June 26, 2006, <http://www.rollingstone.com/reviews/ album/9999948/review/10681153/a_city_by_the_light_divided> (January 9, 2008).

16. Suresh Mohapatra, "Iconic Local DJ Les Aaron's 'New Music Sunday' Rolls On," *Inside STL*, August 2, 2007, <http://www.insidestl.com/stlmusic/index.php?storyid=199> (February 5, 2008).

Further Reading

Books

Burlingame, Jeff. *Kurt Cobain: "Oh Well, Whatever, Nevermind."* Berkeley Heights, N.J.: Enslow Publishers, Inc., 2006.

Schaefer, A. R. *Making a First Recording.* Minneapolis: Capstone Press, 2004.

Skancke, Jennifer. *The History of Indie Rock.* Detroit, Mich.: Lucent Books, 2007.

Web Sites

Alternative Press—A music magazine that follows the latest in alternative rock.
<http://www.altpress.com>

All Music Guide—A site that offers information about all sorts of bands.
<http://www.allmusic.com>

mtvU—The Web site for MTV's college cable channel.
<http://www.mtvu.com>

Index